Ambrose Bierce: The Life and Mysterious Disappearance of the Famous American Author

By Charles River Editors

A portrait of Bierce

About Charles River Editors

Charles River Editors provides superior editing and original writing services across the digital publishing industry, with the expertise to create digital content for publishers across a vast range of subject matter. In addition to providing original digital content for third party publishers, we also republish civilization's greatest literary works, bringing them to new generations of readers via ebooks.

Sign up here to receive updates about free books as we publish them, and visit Our Kindle Author Page to browse today's free promotions and our most recently published Kindle titles.

Introduction

Ambrose Bierce (1842-disappeared 1914)

"History is an account, mostly false, of events, mostly unimportant, which are brought about by rulers, mostly knaves, and soldiers, mostly fools." – Ambrose Bierce

Satirical commentary, memoirs from the agony of war, and horror stories of the supernatural have existed in literature since the beginning of the written word, and in virtually all global societies. The most lauded and familiar examples known to 21st century readers are emblematic of vast literary industries in comparison to previous eras. With an astonishing number of authors at liberty to self-publish and the rapid expansion of the relatively recent film industry, the world has never before seen such a vast expression of such genres. However, as epic film music can often trace its roots back to the Romantic movement of the 1800s, so can the written word. Mark Twain, a preeminent, globally-admired satirist, shared the stage with such wits as Britain's Oscar Wilde, delivering barb after barb laced with the two-edged charm of the old American South.

Nearer the end of the 19th century, Stephen Crane penned *The Red Badge of Courage*, considered the definitive novel on the American Civil War. These, and the ironically inventive horror stories penned by Edgar Allan Poe and the next century's H.P. Lovecraft, remain popular in the West's canon. Examples of these early authors are taught in the American school curriculum, having acquired distinction by the passing of time, often serving as plot and stylistic foundations for new works.

One author who is less frequently mentioned among these iconic literary figures of war, horror, acidic poetry, and social satire, is Ambrose Gwinnet Bierce, a journalist, poet, short-story writer, novelist, fabulist, and writing master who embodied the literary affections of all three. As a satirist, Bierce was famously dubbed the "Mark Twain of the North."[1] Inclusion of the "North," however, embodies several points of dissimilarity from the wit of Twain; sharp and lightning-clever like his counterpart from Missouri, Bierce the Ohioan made no pretense to Southern charm or allowed any room for a nuanced interpretation of his remarks. Once atop his profession, Bierce's venom was spewed at virtually everyone, in almost every walk of life. Any figure of public note in San Francisco came to know him as "Bitter Bierce,"[2] or by his initials, which in public life were often translated as "Almighty God Bierce."[3]

From the early years of childhood, the hated iconoclast took on the mission of telling the truth to all people at all times, "as he understood it."[4] Further, with an extreme measure of suspicion developed through numerous betrayals, he freed his diatribes from all moral restraints as expressed by denominational religion or, in most cases, societal taste and custom. The great bulk of his personal and professional life was spent under the motto, "nothing matters."[5] However, in his crusades against self-appointed moralists and those in positions of power, a great deal seemed to matter. Bierce fiercely promoted his ideal of perfection in writing, and fostered several young talents, among them Jack London, George Sterling, and H.L. Mencken.

As a war author, Bierce is the only one of the great literary figures who actually served as a front-line soldier in the American Civil War. Walt Whitman and Twain were somewhat removed from the conflict by comparison. Twain, in fact, "dabbled"[6] at being a soldier before deserting his Confederate unit. Bierce's often metaphysical and supernatural-tinged memoirs of his war service served as the ideal backdrop for the Poe-like "attraction to death in its most bizarre forms"[7] and an affection for the ghost story as a "campfire tale."[8] A master of the "ironic style of

---

[1] John Patrick, Michael Murphy, Ambrose Bierce, The SecularWeb – www.infidels.org/library/modern/john_murphy/ambrosebierce.jtml
[2] American Literature, Ambrose Bierce – www.americanliterature.com/author/ambrose-bierce/bio-books-stories
[3] American Literature
[4] Poetry Foundation, , Ambrose Bierce – www.poetryfoundation.org/poems-and-poets/detail/ambrose-bierce
[5] American Literature
[6] Jim McWilliams, New York Times, Dickinson State University, Ambrose Bierce's Civil War, , Dec. 17, 2003 – www.opinionator.blogs.nytimes.com/2013/12/17/ambrose-bierces-war/?_r=O
[7] Poetry Foundation
[8] Terrance Rafferty, New York Times, Ambrose Bierce: The Man and His Demons, 2011 – www.nytimes.com/2011/10/30/books/reviews/ambrose-bierce-the-man-and-his-demons.html?_r=o

the grotesque,"[9] he outstripped even Poe in the minds of many readers as "the blackest of black humorists."[10] H.P. Lovecraft, the most prominent author of the macabre in the early part of the following century, described Bierce's work as "grim and savage,"[11] but other critics disagree, citing the "detached, oddly companionable"[12] personality of the storytelling that made the horror all the more penetrating. Indeed, many 20th and 21st century novels, short stories, films, and television serials have drawn their success, squarely from Bierce's models.

In the end, Ambrose Bierce wrote the most interesting story of all by disappearing from the world in a final late-life Mexican adventure, amidst that country's revolution. A new theory of his demise emerges with each passing year, one more colorful than the last. However, despite multiple investigations into his last known whereabouts and the manner of his death, the answer is less sure than ever before.

Ambrose Bierce: The Life and Mysterious Disappearance of the Famous American Author chronicles the author's controversial life and speculated about how he vanished. Along with pictures of important people, places, and events, you will learn about Ambrose Bierce like never before, in no time at all.

---

[9] American Literature
[10] Library of America, Ambrose Bierce, The Devil's, Dictionary, Tales and Memoirs – www.loa.org'books/347-the-devils-dictionary-tales-memoirs
[11] American Literature{in his}
[12] Terrance Rafferty, NY Times

Ambrose Bierce: The Life and Mysterious Disappearance of the Famous American Author
About Charles River Editors
Introduction
   Chapter 1: Early Years
   Chapter 2: The War Years
   Chapter 3: A New Direction
   Chapter 4: Writing Highs, Personal Lows
   Chapter 5: The Final Act
   Online Resources
   Bibliography

Chapter 1: Early Years

"Childhood: the period of human life intermediate between the idiocy of infancy and the folly of youth - two removes from the sin of manhood and three from the remorse of age." – Ambrose Bierce

Ambrose Gwinnett Bierce was born in the rural hamlet of Horse Cave, Ohio, on June 24th, 1842, in Meigs County. As the 10th of 13 children born to Marcus Aurelius and Laura Sherwood Bierce, Ambrose grew up in Kociusko County, Indiana. All of the children, according to their father's wishes, were given names beginning with the letter "A."

Bierce's home environment growing up reflected the larger atmosphere of the region, which one historian called "a hotbed of revivalist frenzy."[13] Between a strict upbringing involving frequent corporal punishment, what he took as a distant and insufficient bond with his mother, and a suppressive religious community, he grew up "suspicious, introverted, and resistant to authority."[14] Bierce later applied this resistance to anyone who applied moral pressure, lied to, or withheld information from him, from the most trivial instances to matters touching the core of his larger life-view. As a child, he is said to have described his parents as "unwashed savages,"[15] and all but cut his mother off when the Santa Claus scandal was revealed to him as a young child. Over this, he claims to have "proceeded to detest my deceivers with all my might and main."[16]

Such a familial repudiation at such an early age was to become emblematic of a lifelong resentment of his upbringing, filled as it was with terrifying sermons intended to frighten children that lived in a "small-minded America."[17] Looking back in his later years, Bierce referred to his younger self as a "crusading idealist in my green and salad days."[18]

Although he moved with his family to Walnut Creek in 1846, close to the county seat of Warsaw, Indiana, the first of many relocations, the tone of his environment remained largely the same. Whatever Bierce's relationship with his father, he claims that the greatest influence of his youth came from the "farmhouse library"[19] that the elder Bierce had painstakingly assembled. From the available works, he gained an abiding love of literature and history. This helped him to prepare for high school, which he attended in Warsaw before eventually running away from home at the age of 15 and blaming his mother for "not loving him enough."[20] For the rest of his

---

[13] Steffany Ann Goldberg, The Smart Set, Pertinent and Impertinent, To the Devil's Dictionary at 100 – www.thesmartset.com/article09261101
[14] Allen Guelzo, Civil War Times Magazine, Historynet, Ambrose' Bierce's Civil War, One Man's Morbid Vision – www.historynet.com/ambrose-bierces-civil-war-one-mans-morbid-vision.html
[15] Steffany Ann Goldberg
[16] Steffany Ann Goldberg
[17] Steffany Ann Goldberg
[18] Allen Guelzo
[19] Ambrose Bierce.org, Timeline – www.ambrosebierce.org/timeline8.html
[20] Roy Morris, the Washington Post, Ambrose Bierce – www.washingtonpost.com/wp-srv/style/longterm/books/chap/bierce.htm

life, Bierce almost entirely avoided his family, gathered few friends, rarely participated in social occasions, and never associated with a school again. Fortunately, he had one hero left - General Lucius Verus Bierce, his uncle, agreed to take him in when the family dynamic collapsed.

Lucius Verus Bierce

Shyness was nowhere to be found within the Bierce family, and General Bierce was no exception. Originally a lawyer and politician born in Connecticut, he appointed himself as Commander-in-Chief of the Canada-Patriot War, without argument. When he heard that his father was ill, he is said to have walked 1,800 miles to see him alive once more, or so says the legend. The general was a celebrity in his state, having served as mayor of Akron for four terms. As a military figure, he was archetypal and well-connected. Among his colleagues was John Brown of Harper's Ferry fame, to whom General Bierce furnished weapons.

John Brown

Strongly anti-slavery, Ambrose adopted the general as the perfect model, admiring his "socialism, oratorical skills, public service, and social activism."[21] Biographer Roy Morris describes this as the most important transformation to Bierce's professional life: "Youth sees the nasty world stretched out before him,"[22] pointing to a military path as the perfect fit for one so "colorful [and] combative."[23]

---

[21] Ambrose Bierce.org
[22] Roy Morris, the Washington Post
[23] Roy Morris, the Washington Post

The heroic life of a soldier did not come at once. The young Bierce trudged through one mundane job after another, into the late 1850s. From time spent as a bricklayer, to working in an ice cream parlor, an oyster bar, a dry goods store, and a tavern, the directionless adolescent remained purposeless. According to town historian Maurice Fink, clients who observed Bierce's varied incarnations as a junior merchant described him as a "queer and different"[24] young man. Fink adds that most who followed his progress gave him a "poor chance"[25] to make good as a man of prospects.

Career preparation, however, began to point in the right direction when Bierce entered into an apprenticeship with a printer at the Northern Indianan. A rudimentary preparation for his future associations with national newspapers and magazines was formed there, although he could scarcely have known it at the time. It was there his sense for the structure of writing and literary form was aroused for the first time.

Chapter 2: The War Years

"Politics: A strife of interests masquerading as a contest of principles. The conduct of public affairs for private advantage." – Ambrose Bierce

With the situation changing in the tension across the country, Bierce entered the Kentucky Military Institute two years later. The Institute was among the oldest and most revered military academies in the United States. There, Bierce delved into military subjects, including topographical engineering. Having taken well to his first taste of experience with the armed forces, he left the Institute on the eve of the Civil War in 1860, and returned to Indiana. There, he joined one of the companies of Marines formed and equipped by his uncle, enlisting on April 19th, 1861. He eventually landed in Company C of the 9th Indiana, with which he would experience his first battle. By this time, he had fully adopted General Bierce's passion against slavery. In later memoirs, he comments that, as a young man still in his teenage years, "I was sufficiently zealous for freedom in order to engage in a few years' battle for its promotion."[26]

Bierce's enlistment on behalf of the Union came only a few days after President Lincoln's general call for volunteers. Soon promoted to Lieutenant with Company C, his first perception of battle in February of 1862 was not those one might expect from the inexperienced. To Bierce's astonishment, the half-hearted commitment of some in authority served as a second great disillusioning, as he witnessed Union officers fleeing the battlefield. In his later recollections, he suggests that his "idealism died that day and was replaced by cynicism."[27] Military or otherwise, his professional course was set that day toward a public literary assault on a "world of fools and rogues, blinded with superstition, tormented with envy, consumed with vanity, selfish, cruel,

---

[24] Roy Morris, the Washington Post
[25] Roy Morris, the Washington Post
[26] Allen Guelzo
[27] Spartacus Educational, Ambrose Bierce – www.spartacus-educational.com/USABierce.htm

cursed with illusions–frothing mad."[28]

Bierce appeared to lack the typical human fear of death, and that observation held up well in battle, especially since he happened to be on hand for the biggest battle in American history at the time. In April 1862, after Union General Ulysses S. Grant captured Fort Henry and Fort Donelson months earlier, Confederate General Albert Sidney Johnston, widely considered the Confederacy's best general, concentrated his forces in northern Georgia and prepared for a major offensive that culminated with the biggest battle of the war to that point, the Battle of Shiloh. On the morning of April 6, Johnston directed an all out attack on Grant's army around Shiloh Church, and though Grant's men had been encamped there, they had failed to create defensive fortifications or earthworks. They were also badly caught by surprise. With nearly 45,000 Confederates attacking, Johnston's army began to steadily push Grant's men back toward the river.

As fate would have it, the Confederates may have been undone by friendly fire at Shiloh. Johnston advanced out ahead of his men on horseback while directing a charge near a peach orchard when he was hit in the lower leg by a bullet that historians now widely believe was fired by his own men. Nobody thought the wound was serious, including Johnston, who continued to aggressively lead his men and even sent his personal physician to treat wounded Union soldiers taken captive. But the bullet had clipped an artery, and shortly after being wounded Johnston began to feel faint in the saddle. With blood filling up his boot, Johnston unwittingly bled to death. The delay caused by his death, and the transfer of command to subordinate P.G.T. Beauregard, bought the Union defenders critical time on April 6.

In *What I Saw of Shiloh*, Bierce wrote of the first day of the battle:

"The morning of Sunday, the sixth day of April, 1862, was bright and warm. Reveille had been sounded rather late, for the troops, wearied with long marching, were to have a day of rest. The men were idling about the embers of their bivouac fires; some preparing breakfast, others looking carelessly to the condition of their arms and accouterments, against the inevitable inspection; still others were chaffing with indolent dogmatism on that never-failing theme, the end and object of the campaign. Sentinels paced up and down the confused front with a lounging freedom of mien and stride that would not have been tolerated at another time. A few of them limped unsoldierly in deference to blistered feet. At a little distance in rear of the stacked arms were a few tents out of which frowsy-headed officers occasionally peered, languidly calling to their servants to fetch a basin of water, dust a coat or polish a scabbard. Trim young mounted orderlies, bearing dispatches obviously unimportant, urged their lazy nags by devious ways amongst the men, enduring with unconcern their good humored raillery, the penalty of superior station. Little

---

[28] Spartacus Educational

negroes of not very clearly defined status and function lolled on their stomachs, kicking their long, bare heels in the sunshine, or slumbered peacefully, unaware of the practical waggery prepared by white hands for their undoing.

"Presently the flag hanging limp and lifeless at headquarters was seen to lift itself spiritedly from the staff. At the same instant was heard a dull, distant sound like the heavy breathing of some great animal below the horizon. The flag had lifted its head to listen. There was a momentary lull in the hum of the human swarm; then, as the flag drooped the hush passed away. But there were some hundreds more men on their feet than before; some thousands of hearts beating with a quicker pulse.

"Again the flag made a warning sign, and again the breeze bore to our ears the long, deep sighing of iron lungs. The division, as if it had received the sharp word of command, sprang to its feet, and stood in groups at "attention." Even the little blacks got up. I have since seen similar effects produced by earthquakes; I am not sure but the ground was trembling then. The mess-cooks, wise in their generation, lifted the steaming camp-kettles off the fire and stood by to cast out. The mounted orderlies had somehow disappeared. Officers came ducking from beneath their tents and gathered in groups. Headquarters had become a swarming hive.

"The sound of the great guns now came in regular throbbings - the strong, full pulse of the fever of battle. The flag flapped excitedly, shaking out its blazonry of stars and stripes with a sort of fierce delight. Toward the knot of officers in its shadow dashed from somewhere - he seemed to have burst out of the ground in a cloud of dust - a mounted aide-de-camp, and on the instant rose the sharp, clear notes of a bugle, caught up and repeated, and passed on by other bugles, until the level reaches of brown fields, the line of woods trending away to far hills, and the unseen valleys beyond were "telling of the sound," the farther, fainter strains half drowned in ringing cheers as the men ran to range themselves behind the stacks of arms. For this call was not the wearisome "general" before which the tents go down; it was the exhilarating assembly," which goes to the heart as wine and stirs the blood like the kisses of a beautiful woman. Who that has heard it calling to him above the grumble of great guns can forget the wild intoxication of its music?"

The Battle of Shiloh lasted two days, but the battle over the battle had just begun. Grant's army swept the Confederates from the field on the second day, with nearly 24,000 combined casualties among the Union and Confederate forces. Usually the winner of a major battle is hailed as a hero, but Grant was hardly a winner at Shiloh. The Battle of Shiloh took place before costlier battles at places like Antietam and Gettysburg, so the extent of the casualties at Shiloh shocked the nation. Moreover, at Shiloh the casualties were viewed as needless; Grant was pilloried for allowing the Confederates to take his forces by surprise, as well as the failure to build defensive earthworks and fortifications, which nearly resulted in a rout of his army. Speculation again arose that Grant had a drinking problem, and some even assumed he was drunk during the battle. Though the Union won, it was largely viewed that their success owed to the heroics of General Sherman in rallying the men and Don Carlos Buell arriving with his army, and General Buell was happy to receive the credit at Grant's expense.

Buell

Bierce was serving under General Buell and Hazen, and on the morning of the second day, he led a platoon of riflemen over the previous day's battlefield. In later recollections of Shiloh as a "terrifying experience,"[29] it was this sweep of the field, out of combat, that shocked him the most. The grotesque carnage deeply affected him, and even the assault on nature, the trees filled with shot and "grape," left a disturbing impression. He wrote of what he saw, "In a few moments we had passed out of the singular oasis that bad so marvelously escaped the desolation of battle, and now the evidences of the previous days struggle were present in profusion. The ground was tolerably level here, the forest less dense, mostly clear of undergrowth, and occasionally opening out into small natural meadows. Here and there were small pools - mere discs of rainwater with a tinge of blood. Riven and torn with cannon-shot, the trunks of the trees protruded bunches of splinters like hands, the fingers above the wound interlacing with those below. Large branches had been lopped, and hung their green heads to the ground, or swung critically in their netting of vines, as in a hammock. Many had been cut clean off and their masses of foliage seriously impeded the progress of the troops. The bark of these trees, from the root upward to a height of ten or twenty feet, was so thickly pierced with bullets and grape that one could not have laid a hand on it without covering several punctures. None had escaped. How the human body survives a storm like this must be explained by the fact that it is exposed to it but a few moments at a time, whereas these grand old trees had had no one to take their places, from the rising to the going down of the sun. Angular bits of iron, concavo-convex, sticking in the sides of muddy depressions, showed where shells had exploded in their furrows. Knapsacks, canteens, haversacks distended with soaken and swollen biscuits, gaping to disgorge, blankets beaten into the soil by the rain, rifles with bent barrels or splintered stocks, waist-belts, hats and the omnipresent sardine-box - all the wretched debris of the battle still littered the spongy earth as far as one could see, in every direction. Dead horses were everywhere; a few disabled caissons, or limbers, reclining on one elbow, as it were; ammunition wagons standing disconsolate behind four or six sprawling mules. Men? There were men enough; all dead, apparently, except one, who lay near where I had halted my platoon to await the slower movement of the line - a Federal sergeant, variously hurt, who had been a fine giant in his time. He lay face upward, taking in his breath in convulsive, rattling snorts, and blowing it out in sputters of froth which crawled creamily down his cheeks, piling itself alongside his neck and ears. A bullet had clipped a groove in his skull, above the temple; from this the brain protruded in bosses, dropping off in flakes and strings. I had not previously known one could get on, even in this unsatisfactory fashion, with so little brain. One of my men, whom I knew from a womanish fellow, asked if he should put his bayonet through him. Inexpressibly shocked by the cold-blooded proposal, I told him I thought not; it was unusual, and too many were looking."

Worse was to come as Bierce led his platoon into an ambush. His memoirs recount the sensations of the day, in which the forest seemed to "flame up…hot hissings…the sickening spat of lead against flesh."[30] Such encounters were to serve as some of Bierce's greatest tales in the

---

[29] New World Encyclopedia Britannica, Ambrose Bierce, American Author – www.britannica.com/biography/Ambrose_Bierce

years to come as a war writer. This single battle became fodder for volumes of "elegiac"[31] expression, once out of the service. He also demonstrated considerable resolve in the battle at Murfreesboro, and in the Battle of Philippi, sometimes referred to as the Battle of Rich Mountain. In this conflict, Bierce saved the life of his commanding officer, Major Braden, under fire. The local press of his home region picked up the story, and the *Indiana Press* trumpeted the achievements of the state's native son, "in the open view of the enemy,"[32] They further reported that Bierce acted heroically as bullets were "falling around him like hail."[33] Two months later, the "troubled teen"[34] of only two years prior, now a distinguished junior officer, found himself assigned to General George McClellan in West Virginia.

McClellan

With a background in topographical engineering, Bierce eventually reenlisted at the reduced rank of sergeant to practice his cartographic skills. He went on to spend a great deal of time in

---

[30] Jim McWilliams
[31] Spartacus Educational
[32] Jim McWilliams
[33] Jim McWilliams
[34] Roy Morris, the Washington Post

the years between 1861 and 1867 assigned to the staff of General William Babcock Hazen, after his stint with the 9th Indiana, and Buell's Army of the Ohio. Few positions in the Civil War came under the heading of a non-combatant, and as Bierce "surveyed landscape [and] prepared detailed maps"[35] for the general, he was a fully committed front-line soldier. Rising again to the status of a young officer, and in need of a hero, Bierce took to Hazen in much the same way he had to General Bierce. One historian suggests that Hazen, considered to be a skillful man by his junior officer, "spun a gruff, fatherly spell"[36] over his subordinates, and that the young Lieutenant warmed to it instantly, calling the general "My master in the art of war."[37] During these years, he is said to have fought bravely in many of the fiercest conflicts after Shiloh and the Siege of Corinth, including Chickamauga, and with Sherman in his march through the South. He fought in the Battle of Stones River as well.

Hazen

Several literary gems emerged from Bierce's personal experience at Chickamauga in

---

[35] Ambroce Bierce.org
[36] Allen Guelzo
[37] Allen Guelzo

September of 1863. Serving in the Union army commanded by General William Rosecrans, he crossed the south as Confederate forces were pursued from Chattanooga in central Tennessee into northern Georgia. In a general strategy, however, the commander erred by separating Union strength into three prongs in an attempt to encapsulate the enemy. This left the invading Union force unable to withstand a strong, centralized counterattack. It was a stubborn Lieutenant Bierce who rode into Union lines at the weakest point to stem the Confederate surge and fill the gap. One of Bierce's most noted stories grew out of the Chickamauga experience, entitled simply, *Chickamauga*. In a typical infusion of horror with the supernatural, Bierce depicts a young boy attempting to play with the ghosts of soldiers. In November of that year, Bierce also fought at the Battle of Missionary Ridge, which broke the Confederate siege of Chattanooga.

In December of 1863, Bierce received his first rest from the war when he received a furlough to return home. Observers were never certain, however, that he desired such a reprieve from further action. Once back in Indiana, he became engaged to a young woman he had courted before his initial enlistment, but said little over the years about the nature of this relationship. He returned to the war in February of 1864, only to be wounded in the battle of Kennesaw Mountain, where he was shot in the head by a Confederate sniper. This was to affect, and eventually truncate, his time with the Union army. As in the case of Pickett's Mill, Bierce was leading a skirmish line at the time of his wounding. It was a severe injury, as the bullet hit his left temple, "grooved its way"[38] underneath the skin, and lodged itself behind the left ear. The shell remained in Bierce's head permanently, as it was far too dangerous to remove with any known surgical procedures. By the time he returned to Indiana on medical leave, his fiancée had called off the engagement, and he had no further wish than to return to action. Once sufficiently recovered, at least in terms of outward behavior, he was cleared to report back to Georgia.

A similarly haunting work resulted from the battle known as Pickett's Mill, which took place on May 27th of 1864. Bierce, in retrospect, titled it *The Crime at Pickett's Mill*. In conflicts such as the Civil War, the rank and file soldier rarely knew anything of the overall situation on the field. The subordinate officer often knew little more of enemy strength or position. At Pickett's Mill, General William Tecumseh Sherman and General Joseph E. Johnston's armies collided in Dallas, Georgia. Bierce's unit assaulted a Confederate line, and owing to thick underbrush and a general confusion of tactical aims, failed to advance, leaving them entirely exposed to the enemy. In the slaughter that ensued, 467 of Bierce's men were killed or wounded in a 45-minute period.

Despite all of the harrowing action Bierce had seen, boredom began to set in. In October of 1864, he and a small group of fellow soldiers allegedly sneaked out of camp, were fired on by a Confederate patrol, and taken captive along the Coosa River. Lodged at a local farmhouse by his captors, he managed to escape, and spent the next three days eluding capture. Reaching Union lines on the fourth, he reportedly "collapsed in a dead faint."[39] Although the experience would

---

[38] Jim McWilliams

result in a later essay entitled *Four Days in Dixie*, the experience did him little good. As his unit marched back to Tennessee, he was held out of the battles of Franklin and Nashville due to his medical condition, which worsened as the campaign proceeded. The shell lodged within his skull caused frequent fainting spells, without any apparent cause or warning. Medical personnel dictated that he not be subjected to "exposure, excitement, or excessive fatigue."[40] As for Bierce's rudimentary self-diagnosis, he said that it felt like his head had "broken like a walnut."[41] He added, on a more serious note, that the old Bierce was dead after "seeing the elephant," a common term for being in combat.[42]

Discrepancies exist as to the remainder of Bierce's military service. Some claim that he was not discharged at all, despite lingering effects from his head wound, and that he was transferred, instead, to South Carolina. There, he is said to have joined the march toward Richmond with Sherman, but no records exist that would corroborate such a theory. The surgeon for the 71st Ohio Volunteers, C.T. Hoagland, swears to have declared him unfit in January of 1865, and added in his notes that Bierce "cannot be subjected to severe mental or physical exertion."[43] None of his future writings referred to the Carolinas as they did to his other actions, and records allegedly written by Bierce in the journal/notebook from that region suffer from atrocious spelling, a side-effect he never experienced in his life and one he would never have tolerated.

Bierce was, without a doubt, forced to resign on January 25th, as the surgeon claimed. His request for promotion to the rank of captain was denied at a time when it was his intention to continue, but in forced retirement, he was officially granted the rank of Brevet Major. In the same month, he was mustered out of the army in Huntsville, Alabama, and became a treasury agent there, a claim that is disputed by some. Other reports suggest that Bierce's term as an agent was spent in Selma, and that it was not altogether peaceful. In one reported incident, his steamboat, loaded with confiscated cotton, was attacked by bandits on the Tombigbee River. Bierce fought them off handily, according to local accounts.

Chapter 3: A New Direction

"Doubt is the father of invention." – Ambrose Bierce

1865 is usually cited as the year in which Bierce began to write memoirs of the war and the beginnings of later published works, in a personal journal. The entries are believed to be the first examples of his serious writings taken from personal experience.

Not to be shut out from the military life, however, Bierce rejoined General Hazen after the war, in an expedition into Indian Territory, again as a mapmaker. By 1867, he reached San

---

[39] Jim McWilliams
[40] Jim McWilliams
[41] Ambrose Bierce Letters Project, University of Cincinnati – www.lipapps.libraries.uc.edu/exhibits/ambrose-bierce-2/
[42] Jim McWilliams
[43] Matthew C. O'Brien, Ambrose Bierce and the Civil War: 1865, *American Literature* Vol. 48 No. 3 (Nov. 1976) Duke University Press, p. 380

Francisco, and remained there as an employee of the U.S. Mint through 1871. Thus began his writing career, with the West Coast's most cultured city as a vessel and backdrop.

    Attention to Bierce's writing ability began as a response to his editorials and essays, some of which he sent to various city newspapers. Many of his submissions were comic sketches, without the later weightiness of his work. In 1868, the *San Francisco Newsletter* took him on staff, not only as a contributing writer but eventually as managing editor for the column entitled *The Town Crier*. From what some have described as his "literary pulpit,"[44] he proceeded to take on anyone in the city holding a position of leadership, with the intent to "savage the city's hypocrites and political scoundrels."[45] Bierce took a special relish in attacking social reformers and liberal politicians, and advocated what would serve as a starkly conservative regimen in any century, including a "vigilant censorship of the press [and] a firm hand upon the church."[46] Against all forms of socialism, Bierce recommended strict supervision of all public meetings, amusements, overall command of the railroad system, the telegraph, and all other communications, presumably including hand-written letters.

    No one was spared the wrath of the new journalist. In obtaining a forum from which to lambaste all that had troubled his childhood, he assaulted religion and fellow writers whenever possible with Twain-like witticisms, albeit without the grace of a Southern veneer. Missionaries, he described as "those who would beat a dog with a crucifix."[47] He compared the observance of the Sabbath day as "a weekly festival having its origin in the act that God made the world in six days, and was arrested on the seventh."[48] Religion itself he characterized as "a daughter of Hope and Fear, explaining to Ignorance the nature of the unknowable."[49] He attacked one journalist as suffering from an unhealed wound – "his mouth."[50] Politicians often got the worst of it, as Bierce berated their profession as a "strife of interests masquerading as a contest of principles."[51] His personal experience with lawyers saw to it they were not to be spared; no stranger to litigation, he defined the process of bringing lawsuits as "a machine you go into as a pig and come out as a sausage."[52]

    The city of San Francisco was in the midst of what one historian labeled an "artistic renaissance"[53] at Bierce's arrival, and it was the perfect time for such an agitating columnist to

---

[44] Ambrose Bierce.org
[45] Ambrose Bierce.org
[46] Spartacus Educational
[47] Dr. Weirdre, The Wickedest Man in San Francisco: Ambrose Bierce, Historical Essay – www.foundsf.org/index.php?title=The-Wickedest-Man-in-San-Francisco:_Ambrose_Bierce
[48] Brainy Quotes
[49] Brainy Quotes
[50] Dr. Weirdre
[51] Gary Galles, Mises Institute, Ambrose Bierce on Politics, Austrian Economics, Freedom, and Peace – www.mises.org/blog/ambrose-bierce-politics
[52] Brainy Quotes
[53] Encyclopaedia Britannica

appear, one addressed by an enemy as "an asthmatic, superstitious, bilious atheist."[54] He reveled in the title of "wickedest man in San Francisco,"[55] and before long, his biting assaults, with such "precise language and moral certitude"[56] achieved a legendary status that went far beyond the city. Major newspapers in New York and London began to include contributions from the American iconoclast. Many mistook his diatribes for raw vanity, when in fact, cynicism was his "life force,"[57] more than a mere attitude or vain quest for fame.

    Through his position, Bierce was able to meet other noted authors and journalists, including Mark Twain, and more importantly, Bret Harte, editor of the *Overland Monthly*. It was to be the *Monthly* that published the first of his stories, entitled *The Haunted Valley,* in 1871. Among other unthinkable devices to the mind of 19th century culture, the grim short story features an axe murder and a transgender love triangle. Filled with insane characters, it was a finely honed attack on what Bierce believed to be the blight of hypocritical Christian charity. Bierce's brand of tragedy and ironic horror produced works such as *The Death of Halpin Frayser*, a Gothic ghost story published in one of San Francisco's well-known publications, The Wave. In a telling autobiographical penchant, the central character is killed by the zombie corpse of his mother.

---

[54] John Patrick, Michael Murphy, The SecularWeb, 1999, Ambrose Bierce – www.infidels.org/library/modern/john-murphy/ambrosebierce.html
[55] Poetry Foundation, Ambrose Bierce – www.poetryfoundation.org/poems-and-poets/details/ambrose-bierce
[56] Ambrose Bierce.org
[57] Steffany Ann Goldberg

Harte

Other featured works of the year's collection included *The Damned Thing*, the story of an inquest held at the cabin of a man who has been hunting an invisible creature, and has apparently been killed by it. *The Moonlit Road*, released later in *Cosmopolitan* magazine, involves murders and communications from the dead through a medium. Bierce's use of the ghost, which he defined as the "outward and visible sign of an inward fear,"[58] evoked an unsettled dread in the reader that he had the supernatural to fear in addition to a grotesque temporal reality, and that the two could mix at a moment's notice. Deemed by many as the best horror writer compared to Poe and H.P. Lovecraft, the addition of war and the isolation of central characters created a surreal sense of the waking dream, "steeped in loneliness and dread."[59] Beyond the story itself, Bierce attempted to infect his reader with a "nothing matters" motto, and set the scene against the "horror of a meaningless universe."[60]

Equally important to content was the perfection of the writing for Bierce, and he pursued

---

[58] Terrance Rafferty
[59] Terrance Rafferty
[60] Poetry Foundation

literary artistry as much as he did dramatic power. His choice of form typically opened with an "abrupt beginning,"[61] employing dark imagery and loose references to time. He strove to avoid being overly descriptive, and the theme of war intertwining with impossible events seemed ever-present. He was often fond of the procedure known as "leonine,"[62] by which a single line of poetry with an internal rhyming scheme is based on an intentional mispronunciation of the words. All of his traits evoked a respect by colleagues worldwide, who hailed him as "a master of pure English."[63] His short stories came to be regarded as some of the best in his century, and he managed a wide array of literary genres with skill.

    At the height of his success in San Francisco, Bierce's life took a turn on Christmas Day of 1871, when he married Mary Ellen "Mollie" Day, a society lady of high pedigree, undoubtedly from a markedly different upbringing. Marriage was problematic for Bierce from the beginning, and he rarely mentioned his new wife. Quips begin to appear, however, such as the ode to women that includes a man's wish that he might fall into her arms rather than into her hands. Love, he defined as being "curable by marriage."[64] He took other children into his circle more readily than he would his own, and often decried the "miseries of married couples [and the] loathsomeness of babies."[65] Life itself was not immune, as Bierce assaulted birth as "the first and direst of all disasters."[66] As for death, he insisted that it is not the end, for "there remains the litigation over the estate."[67]

---

[61] Allengulette.com, Ambrose Bierce – www.allengulette.com/lit/bierce/
[62] New World Encyclopedia
[63] New World Encyclopedia
[64] Brainy Quotes, Ambrose Bierce – wwwbrainyquote.comquotes/authors/ambrose_bierce_2.html
[65] St. Joshi, Dvid E. Schultz, Introduction to A Sole Survivor: Bits of Autobiography by Ambrose Bierce, Knoxville, University of Tennessee, 1998
[66] Brainy Quotes
[67] Brainy Quotes

Mollie Day

In 1872, Bierce resigned from *The Newsletter* and embarked on a three-year honeymoon in England, where he wrote for publications such as *Fun, Figaro*, and the *London Sketchbook*. *The Passing Showman*, written for *Figaro*, attained great popularity. In this year, the first of Bierce's two sons, Day, was born, and the family moved to Bristol, seeking relief from the London climate. Bierce's asthma remained with him through his entire life, and it caused no end of physical discomfort.

By 1873, he published his first book, *The Fiend's Delight*, followed by *Nuggets and Dust*. Growing ever more satirical in his writing, he published *Cobwebs from an Empty Skull* in 1874. In that year, his second son, Leigh, was born. In 1875, the family returned to San Francisco, where daughter Helen was born.

Working with the publication *Argonaut* upon his return, Bierce took over a column entitled *Prattle*, often called *The Prattler*. The ensuing "poetry, quips, anecdotes, stories, and essays"[68] expanded his former genre to a more varied offering of subjects, with the inclusion of "literary

---
[68] Ambrose Bierce.org

gossip,"[69] the forerunner of such popular 20th century columnists. This did not satisfy his lust for opportunities associated with heightened literary quality, and in 1880 he made a drastic decision to take on the general manager position at the Black Hills Gold Mining Company, far from the culture of San Francisco, in the Dakotas. Horrified by the corrupt system to be found there, he wrote that he was demoralized by the many "deceptions and betrayals,"[70] held the move to be one of the worst decisions of his life, and by far the greatest professional blunder of his career.

 Fortunately, he was able to return to San Francisco and the *Prattler*. It was at this time that he began to publish his Civil War writings, the core of his body of work. Simultaneously, he began *The Cynic's Handbook*, which would become better known by its new title, *The Devil's Dictionary*, a collection of "skewering aphorisms."[71] Bierce often spent stretches of time away from home, living in resorts outside the city where his asthma was less severe, and where his family was less present.

 Dance of Death was published in 1877, an odd intertwining of death as a topic and scandalous dancing, in particular, the waltz, as a social ill. The dance form was considered grossly inappropriate in the Victorian era, and Bierce assigned the term "Waltzer" to any woman who practiced betrayal on a man. The various commentaries are shown through a stylistic lens that mixes ancient Greek and Byronic atmospheres. The theme of dance would appear again in one of Bierce's ghostly skeleton stories, *The Major's Tale*. When it comes time for the specter to do his celebrative dance of death over the bodies of the fallen, he stuns his viewers by dancing instead a peace-affirming series of steps.

 Although Crane's *The Red Badge of Courage* is emblematic of his writing on Civil War topics, Bierce's memories were both more real than Crane could ever have devised, and Bierce preceded Crane's legendary work by over a decade. As a horror writer employing the supernatural, the war was used as a backdrop, but the Confederacy was not designated as the true enemy. It was death itself that was cast as the ultimate antagonist, and the man who could cope with it on the battlefield was the hero. To draw the distinction, Bierce employed real memories of officers who killed themselves in battle. In a story of powerful irony entitled *The Affair at Coulter's Notch*, he tells the story of an officer who knowingly has his own house shelled, killing his family.

 In 1882, Bierce wrote for another progressive publication, *The Wasp*. While in possession of this forum, he took aim at British wit Oscar Wilde, who was touring America and lecturing on "the future of art in a philistine world."[72] Whether out of professional jealousy, or as a response to Wilde's criticism of satire as an art form, Bierce exploded in a diatribe against the visitor. Taking Wilde to task for calling himself "le petit roi" (the little king) who could speak on

---

[69] The Free Online Library, Ambrose Bierce (1842-1914) – www.bierce.thefreelibrary.com
[70] Ambrose Bierce.org
[71] Allen Guelzo
[72] Roy Morris

ephemeral subjects such as "the science of the beautiful,"[73] Bierce scalded him with unflattering terms, including "sovereign of the insufferables,"[74] a "dung hill he-hen who would fly with eagles,"[75] and "an ineffable dunce."[76] Following that, he left *The Wasp* for one year, and was surprised to find a dearth of opportunities for work, as he had made so many enemies as an "unforgiving social critic."[77]

---

[73] Roy Morris
[74] Roy Morris
[75] Roy Morris
[76] Roy Morris
[77] Ambrose Bierce.org

Wilde

Chapter 4: Writing Highs, Personal Lows

"What is a democrat? One who believes that the republicans have ruined the country. What is a republican? One who believes that the democrats would ruin the country." – Ambrose Bierce

Bierce's marriage to Mary unraveled after 17 years together, but he found new opportunity for escaping its constraints through his new employer, William Randolph Hearst, owner of the *San Francisco Examiner*. Hearst granted Bierce the leeway with which to reestablish *The Prattler* without editorial interference, and he began, once again, to "spear the usual politicians, charlatans, and literary figures,"[78] now at the sum of $100.00 per week. While the subject of marital dissolution was fresh on his mind, he was famously quoted as saying that divorce would result in "a resumption of diplomatic relations and rectification of boundaries."[79] Despite the iconic remark, Mary and Ambrose would not receive an official decree of divorce for a number of years.

By 1888, his marriage had ended formally, if not legally, and in that year, his son Day ran away from home at the age of 15. From there, Bierce spiraled into a regimen of alcoholism. He claimed that his wife had "willingly"[80] received love letters from a "European admirer,"[81] and wanted no part of her after such a discovery. He was likely hasty in his judgment, but insisted on the separation, regardless. He claimed the greatest source of stress in the marriage to have been his mother-in-law, and he only spoke to Mary again on one or two occasions for the rest of his life. He "cut her off as he had his mother years before,"[82] and never entertained marriage again. Once more deceived in his mind, he continued as a cynic, whose job it was to destroy false goodness and bring about a more true affection between humans. It was something he lamentably not allow in his own life, for fear of further injury.

---

[78] Ambrose Bierce.org
[79] Brainy Quotes
[80] Ambrose Bierce.org
[81] Ambrose Bierce.org
[82] Steffany Ann Goldberg

Hearst

On top of it all, 1889 also brought the death of his eldest son Day. Not yet 18 years of age, his first-born died in a gunfight with a rival who had stolen his fiancée. After they "ran off and married,"[83] Day reportedly confronted him in the street and gunned him down, before turning the gun on himself. Both men were mortally wounded. A stunned Bierce realized that he had never found comfort in any aspect of family life after the army. He had lost his marriage, one of his children, and could no longer accept living in the "materialism of the Gilded Age,"[84] a period of financial boom in late 19th century America. He could not abide white privilege and general Caucasian domination of society, or the juxtaposition of war and servitude. He wrote that although we conquer other races because we are "a race of drunkards and gluttons,"[85] and that we can "thrash them consummately,"[86] we cannot and never will "understand them."[87] In his

---

[83] Ambrose Bierce.org
[84] Allen Guelzo
[85] Dr. Weirdre

own era, he foresaw the first signs of what he took to be an American form of imperialism that would bloom in 20th century conflicts overseas. He was, in general, disgusted by the Grant presidency, and felt the urge to participate in someone else's civil war in a return to the familiar. With all his losses, Bierce is described by Roy Morris as being "profoundly disillusioned, [and that he] spent the next five years struggling to disabuse his fellow Americans of their own cherished ideals."[88] His writing reflected the change, as he sought to distinguish the war experience of the veteran from that of the civilian. In 1890, Bierce wrote his most famous work, *Occurrence at Owl Creek Bridge*, in which a Confederate sympathizer is sentenced to die for attempting to sabotage a bridge. He imagines an inventive and daring escape, and the reader only realizes in the final paragraph that it was a day-dream, and that he will be hanged after all. In the following century, films were made on *Occurrence at Owl Creek Bridge*, one a silent film in the '20s, as well as a French version entitled *La Riviere du Hibou*, and a Gregory Peck classic in the early '80s..

Bierce's *In the Midst of Life: Tales of Soldiers and Civilians*, published in 1892, is considered a masterpiece that explores the "romantic and naïve notions"[89] of war. *Chickamauga*, a story on collateral damage, finds a hearing- and speech-impaired boy playing at war who stumbles upon the dead body of a woman hit by a shell, and must either hide from the reality or find a way to make sense of it. In such stories, Bierce "contests traditional, inherited rhetoric that romanticizes the Civil War,"[90] and by putting the reader in the soldier's shoes, "unveils illusions of glory and heroism."[91] In an apparent reversal toward pacifism, Bierce exposes the civilian's "fundamental miscomprehension"[92] toward war in an attempt to make entering one less likely.

While an author such as Twain uses the romantic language of war against itself, Bierce divests it of all beauty, employing the supernatural element for "manipulation of the reader's viewpoint."[93] For the soldier, Bierce intended his work to serve as an avenue for those seeking to understand their grotesque memories in order to reconcile them with their present. However, according to one analyst of PTSD, they inevitably and endlessly collide with the violent horror that only serves to reaffirm their distance from those of the present. According to Marianne Johnson of Gettysburg College, Bierce falsely sets himself up as a skeptical realist, but in truth, he wrote much more like a "jaded romantic"[94] and a "traumatized soldier."[95]

---

[86] Dr. Weirdre
[87] Dr. Weirdre
[88] Roy Morris
[89] Tim Edwards, eScholarship, University of California, *Transnational American Studies* – The Real Prayer and the Imagined: The War Against Romanticism in Twain, Howells, and Bierce
[90] Peter Morrone, *The Midwest Quarterly*, Questia, The Ethics of Moral Resistance: Ambrose Bierce and General William B. Hazen
[91] Peter Morrone
[92] Peter Morrone
[93] Poetry Foundation
[94] Marianne S. Johnson, Gettysburg College, A Jaded Romantic: Uncovering the True Nature of Ambrose Bierce – www.cupola.gettysburg.edu/compiler/49/
[95] Marianne S. Johnson

Through the following few years, Bierce's asthma worsened, and he was unable to keep many appointments or meet obligations. Fewer short stories were written as he refocused his energies on *The Prattler*. But despite his increasing penchant for reclusive behavior, there were exceptions. In the early 1880s, he took an intense interest in the poetry of a young girl named Lily Walsh, born in England. A deaf-mute, she nevertheless continued a ceaseless correspondence with Bierce on the subject of her literary aspirations. Her father, Miles, became a naturalized American citizen and brought his daughter with him, encouraging and participating in the literary mentoring. She was treated at the Wilkinson School in Berkeley, California, as recommended by Bierce. He supported her writing, and sent critiques for each new example she sent him. Upon Lily's death in 1885 at the age of 13, Bierce continued to correspond with Miles, and carefully tended Lily's grave, commissioning a headstone at St. Mary's Cemetery in Oakland. He wrote an elegant epitaph to have engraved there, but was only allowed to include her name and dates of birth and death.

Following publication of the instantly famous *In the Midst of Life, Tales of Soldiers and Civilians* in 1892, Bierce released *The Monk and the Hangman's Daughter* in the same year, a retelling of a novel penned by German author Richard Voss. The sexuality of death and the appropriate subjugation of desire is explored as a visiting monk falls in love with a young girl, the hangman's daughter, as he watches her dance under a hanging corpse. His process for dealing with such a state of lust, and his punishment for it, is psychologically rich. A large collection of works, *Black Beetles in Amber*, was also released.

HERR RICHARD VOSS

Voss

Hearst reemployed Bierce in 1896 and relocated him to Washington, D.C. for a specific task, perfectly tailored to a bombastic critic of his sort. The Union Pacific and Central Pacific had both received massive loans from the government, and Collis. P. Huntington, owner and president of the South Pacific, introduced a bill in Congress to excuse the entire repayment of 130 million. To oppose this, Hearst turned to his most "lacerating columnist."[96] Taking up temporary residence in the capitol city, which he was fond of addressing as "the seat of misgovernment,"[97] Bierce released a relentless stream of diatribes against the bill and its sponsor. Bierce's work successfully "aroused public wrath,"[98] to such a point that the bill became unfeasible. Huntington went down in defeat and was forced to break up his railroad conglomerate.

Huntington

By 1897, Bierce had again returned to San Francisco, feeling "re-energized"[99] from his triumph on the one hand but lacking the usual zeal for his standard line of attack against the city's noted figures on the other. That Christmas, he sent out a sizeable quantity of Christmas cards to friends, colleagues, and enemies that read, "I wish you a ____Christmas. Fill in the

---

[96] Ambrose Bierce.org
[97] Brainy Quotes
[98] New World Encyclopedia
[99] Ambrose Bierce.org

blank to suit."[100] His correspondence indicates that while he still wrote for Hearst, his only obligation was to work when "I feel like it."[101] Still a crusader for good writing, he often jumped to the defense of abused colleagues. In a notable case, he excoriated famed editor A.F. Naterhouse for publishing a friend's work without including the author's name. Writing to the offended colleague, he referred to Naterhouse as "an all-around sneak."[102]

Health problems continued to beset Bierce, and in 1898 he reported that his asthmatic condition was active "most of the time now…but I'm not going to try anything except the temper of my friends."[103] In that year, he reversed his pacifistic view on the war with Spain after the destruction of *The Maine* in Havana Harbor. Espousing war with Cuba, he changed the title of *Prattler* to *War Topics*, even though he continued to report on the conflict with "waning enthusiasm."[104] This spurred him to request yet another transfer to Washington. At Hearst's approval, Bierce went east once more to write for the *Examiner*, *Cosmopolitan*, and other major publications, and to be entertained by the likes of Theodore Roosevelt and other luminaries. In 1899, *Fantastic Fables* was published, a collection of quick and witty fables that turn dark at the least expected moment. As an example, the Angel of Compassion visits a man who has laughed at the misfortune of the woman he loves. The angel's tear is formed into a hailstone which falls hard on the man's head. The angel does what he first condemned, by laughing at the man's misfortune.

Leigh Bierce, Bierce's second son, died of pneumonia in New York in 1901, and his father went through a patch of dark distraction in which he found trouble in the aftermath of a few published comments. Such trouble was a common occurrence, but this time it involved the president of the United States. Following the publication of a poem about McKinley, he was accused of calling for the president's assassination after the fact, despite his insistence that the poem had an entirely different meaning: "The bullet that pierced Gobel's breast cannot be found in all the west–Good reason, it is speeding here to stretch McKinley on his bier."[105] The poem reflected badly on Hearst for a time, but the magnate stood behind his employee.

Among the only respites from his ceaseless state of anxiety, Bierce spent the summer of 1903 in West Virginia, a part of the country he had known well as a young soldier. The land filled him with "welcome emotion."[106] During this year, he completed *Shapes of Clay*, a collection of poetry that calls to mind the ironically witty style of James Thurber in a later generation, albeit with a more tart delivery and darker purpose.

---

[100] Ambrose Bierce Letters Project
[101] Ambrose Bierce Letters Project
[102] Ambrose Bierce Letters Project
[103] Ambrose Bierce Letters Project
[104] Ambrose Bierce.org
[105] New World Encyclopedia
[106] Ambrose Bierce.org

Almost entirely without family, friends, or professional allies, Bierce fell to drinking again, often with H.L. Mencken as his companion. In 1905, his wife Mary died of sudden heart failure in Los Angeles. Separated, but never officially divorced, she attempted to set Bierce legally free some months before, believing that it was his intention to remarry once in Washington, an inaccurate assumption on her part.

Mencken

With his cynicism at full strength, 1906 saw the publication of his infamous work *The Devil's Dictionary* in its completed form. As a self-appointed "devil," Bierce linked the word to its Greek origin of "slanderer, or accuser."[107] In his version of the cynic's historical lineage, he walked in the shoes of the 5th century cynic Diogenes, who insisted that man must be "free of influence–wealth, power, fame…no allegiances, no state."[108]

One literary historian claimed that Bierce "attacked goodness because he believed in it, and attacked faith because he had lost it."[109] Works such as *A Song of the Gods* and *a Horseman in the Sky* followed, released in a 1907 publication. *Horseman*, one of Bierce's most ironic stories, was among the most widely read after publication. In it, a lonely sentry falls asleep on isolated

---

[107] Steffany Ann Goldberg
[108] Steffany Ann Goldberg
[109] Steffany Ann Goldberg

ground, but is awakened by a colleague to see a Confederate officer on horseback, above, on a ledge. He prepares to shoot, but is held back by a moment of moral hesitation. His solution is to shoot the horse, instead, another reference to collateral damage and crimes against the innocent.

Though he wrote fewer works through 1909, Bierce was still able to publish *The Shadow on the Dial and Other Essays*, a collection of commentary on political dissent and other timeless social issues. In the same year, he wrote his "how to" text for writers, *Write It Right: A Handbook of Literary Faults*, a noted standard for the day. In the same year, Bierce ceased to write for Hearst, and began to set his collected works in order while publishing with Neale Publishing Company. He felt that he had reached the end of his career, and longed to feel the thrill of "change and adventure"[110] one more time. Such an urge grew through the next four years, setting the stage for one of the most romanticized and unexplained disappearances of any celebrity figure from the last two centuries.

Chapter 5: The Final Act

"Death is not the end. There remains the litigation over the estate." – Ambrose Bierce

In the fall of 1913, at the age of 71, Bierce found himself on a train from Washington to the south in a nostalgic revisiting of his old Civil War battlefields. Along the way, he "paid final respects"[111] to what he viewed as the most important, and perhaps, the happiest time in his life, in some perverse interpretation. He wandered his way through Louisiana into Texas, with an eye to the border and southward, and to the simmering revolution taking place there.

Several references to his intentions appeared in final correspondences with those close to him, including a final letter to his niece, Laura. His hope was to apparently join up in some way or other with the Mexican revolutionary Pancho Villa, either as a journalistic observer or actual combatant. In the letter, his disdain for and impatience with the indignities of old age, the suffering of disease, falling down the stairs, and other such accidents of the aged, rang clear. Likewise, he almost glorified the heroic death of a crusader, declaring that being put up against a wall and shot by one's enemies is the grandest way to leave life–"to be a Gringo in Mexico–ah, that is euthanasia."[112] Other items from his last messages shed light on what, to some, appeared as a quixotic, late-life rally. A note that read, "I'm on my way to Mexico because I like the game"[113] was accompanied by a similar sentiment where Bierce jokes about wanting to see "if the Mexicans can shoot straight."[114] In his written testimony to seek "revolutionary Mexico,"[115] he also admitted that, in truth, he was equally in pursuit of an appropriate way to end his life, seeking what he called "the good, kind darkness."[116]

---

[110] Ambrose Bierce.org
[111] Ambrose Bierce.org
[112] IMDb, Ambrose Bierce Biography – www.imdb.com/name/nm0081549/bio?ref_=nm_ov_bio_sm#trivia
[113] Ambrose Bierce Letters Project
[114] Dr Weirdre
[115] Ambrose Bierce.org

Pancho Villa

The last clue to his disappearance across the border read simply, "As to me, I leave here for an unknown destination…I don't know where I shall be next. Guess it doesn't matter much. Adios, Ambrose."[117]

One piece of Bierce's itinerary was deduced from the time in which Villa captured the region of Juarez. It is known that Bierce took the train to El Paso, and through his vast journalistic background, secured press credentials from what historians describe as "more tolerant Constitutional forces."[118] His route to this point and what might have happened to him in the

---

[116] Free Online Library
[117] James McWilliams, Austin Chronicle, May 17, 2002, Devil in the Details, Why is 'Talented Amateur Historian' Leon Day Obsessed with the Death of Ambrose Bierce?

following month is unknown, but the sizeable body of theories seemingly gain a new contribution with each passing year. Some overlap, while others make insufficient logistical sense. Some appear to be in perfect keeping with Bierce's personality and life view, while others paint an uncharacteristic picture.

    Pinning down the day or the precise location at which Bierce crossed the border into Mexico has proved an erratic pursuit. It is possible that the crossing was made at Laredo, which was, at the time, renowned as a dangerous point of entry. The land on the Mexican side was held by Huertistas who depended on anonymity to carry out their revolutionary activities. The last thing the guerilla band wanted was "journalistic scrutiny."[119] If his intent was to follow and interact with the American Press Corps entering the region from Sonoma, Bierce got the jump on them all by a full week. This being the case, he apparently intended to act independently from the beginning, harboring no kinship with, or appreciation for, war correspondents of the era. Having always been in the immediate circle of leadership, Bierce had no intention of standing in a line of observers holding paper and pen, and in fact, sought to establish a direct collegial relationship with Villa and other revolutionary celebrities. Once in Mexico, many reports and mere rumors had Bierce riding, instead, with Venustiano Carranza's guerillas, with in the hope he would eventually find the top man.

---

[118] James McWilliams
[119] James McWilliams

Carranza

Many believe that in the following weeks, Bierce did indeed link up with Villa and establish the relationship he so fondly imagined. It is also believed that this relationship was likely the direct cause of his death. No longer accustomed to being a subservient public figure, it is theorized that Bierce argued with Villa over the procedure for conducting the revolution, tactics, and personal politics. Villa, not known as a graceful recipient of criticism or as a collaborator, is said, according to this theory, to have shot Bierce and left him dead and unburied in the desert. Others believe Villa simply abandoned him there, still alive, to die in the elements. Neither account can be corroborated with any certainty. In September of 1914, Franklin Lane, Secretary of Interior under Woodrow Wilson, launched an unsuccessful effort, funded by the government, to find him. A separate search was conducted by Bierce's daughter, Helen, led by Colonel C.J. Velardi. The family's search failed similarly.

Lane

The most plausible answer to the many inquiries is that Bierce did fight alongside Villa and arrived alive at the Battle of Onijaga on January 11, 1914, only a short distance across the border from the American town of Presidio. His secretary in the United States received a postcard mailed from Chihuahua City, suggesting that Bierce intended to reach Onijaga soon. Biographer Friedrich Katz adds some color to the theory, suggesting Bierce took up a rifle in a skirmish around Tierra Blanca, much in the style he had during the Civil War. Katz further claims that Bierce killed a "federale" at some distance, and was awarded a sombrero by Villa's men in celebration of his marksmanship.

Testimony after the revolution was taken from an American mercenary who claimed to be present at the Battle of Onijaga. According to this alleged eyewitness, Bierce, referred to as the "Old Gringo," was killed in the battle. To reinforce the testimony, a Villista named Ybarra is said to have identified a primitive photo of Bierce, and claims his body was disposed of with hundreds of others which were stacked together and then burned. Still others claim Bierce was only wounded at Onijaga, although his injuries were reported to be severe. According to some reports, Bierce was spotted by a young federale soldier who was running for his life from the breached fort at Onijaga. He was attempting to reach the American border along with several colleagues when he found an "incoherent, moaning gringo."[120] It occurred to the young soldier that he might get better treatment on the other side of the border if he appeared in the company of a "norteamericano."[121] The report claims that the soldier floated Bierce through the river shallows on an old, two-wheeled cart, and that at one point the injured man mumbled his first name. Once across, the soldier was collected with other refugees, and separated from Bierce. From there, everyone was sent by railroad to Marfa for processing. Eventually, according to a secondary source who spoke with the soldier, the delirious gringo, who possessed no papers or identification, and was "nearly comatose,"[122] died. It was claimed that he was one of many buried without markers at the old Camp Marfa Cemetery. This account of Bierce's death was first publicized long after in the 1990 *Big Bend Sentinel,* and later in the *Journal of Big Bend Studies.* The narrative of the story was related to Abelardo Sanchez of Lancaster, California by a hitchhiker of approximately 60 years of age. The wanderer, telling the story in 1957, claimed to have been a federale from many decades past.

How the story came to him is unclear, but many still disagree with its entire premise, as Bierce is reported by some to have been fighting well into April of 1914, several months after Onijaga. An alternate theory proposes that instead of dying at Marfa, Bierce was killed in action near the village of Icamole. The former story continues, claiming that after being returned to American soil by the Mexican federal officer, Bierce recovered sufficiently to cross the border yet again. There, he rode with a federale mule train near the village of Icamole, where it was raided by Villa. Most of the unit survived the assault, but Bierce and an Indian muleteer were killed.

An investigation conducted several years later by James H. Wilkins was based on his hope to interview several witnesses regarding a photograph snapped of what some claim to be Bierce's unburied corpse, with a few possessions laying strewn around the body. Wilkins worked for the *San Francisco Bulletin,* and through a two-year period ending in March of 1920, maintained a steady correspondence with Padre Jaime Leinert, Priest of a church that included Sierra Mojada. Although many believed the photo to be of dubious value, the cleric insisted that Ambrose Bierce was killed in Sierra Mojada by "suspicious government soldiers."[123] Padre Leinert himself erected a monument to Bierce in the Sierra Mojada Cemetery. As an epitaph, he instructed the stone should read, "Very trustworthy witnesses suppose that here lie the remains of Ambrose Gwinett Bierce, 1842-1914–a famous American writer and journalist who on suspicion of being a spy was executed and buried at this place."[124] Nonetheless, Wilkins suspected that Bierce was put in front of a firing squad and executed in the village of Icamole at a later time in 1915.

---

[120] Forrest Gander, Brown University, the Paris Review, The Many Deaths of Ambrose Bierce, Oct. 17, 2014 – www.theparisreview.org/blog/2014/10/17/very-trustworthy-witnesses/
[121] Forrest Gander
[122] Forrest Gander
[123] Forrest Gander
[124] Forrest Gander

According to the oldest man at Sierra Mojada, decades after the alleged incident, he clearly remembered the incident in his youth, observing that the "gringo" was known at the time as El Ruso. Another guerilla, riding with Torelio Ortega, one of Villa's commanders, insisted that the Old Gringo had come through the village carrying maps, and asking local citizens where he might find trails that would lead him to Pancho Villa's army. The story goes on to say that some of those questioned by Bierce were federale supporters. He was allegedly taken prisoner as a suspected spy and summarily executed. It is also said that following the execution, personal effects, including two envelopes addressed to Ambrose Bierce, were found in the dead man's possession.

Another school of thought suggests that Bierce passed through Mexico but never stopped there to engage in any way with the revolution in Mexico. Instead, he traveled the length of the country and went on to Central America. A few have pointed out Bierce's similarity to writer and journalist Francisco Goldman, suggesting that the former had found an "occult serum"[125] to make himself de-age into a younger man.

Others feel certain that Bierce's death was a suicide, or that his geriatric adventure ended at an unknown sanitarium. Proponents of the suicide alternative believe he went east and north, and that his life's "fitful fever ended in a Grand Canyon suicide…one bullet and a long fall."[126] Bierce had openly proposed suicide many times, and had threatened it repeatedly. Those who knew him personally tended to believe in every one of his announced intentions. The idea that the entire Mexican adventure was a grand journalistic hoax, ideal fodder for best-selling memoirs and tall tales, was in favor for a time. James McWilliams suggests in the *Austin Chronicle* that the idea of a hoax did not lie outside of Bierce's parameters. For the average citizen, he suggests, a hoax is a crime, but to a journalist who writes suspenseful horror stories, it is "an art form."[127]

New theories of Bierce's itinerary and eventual demise emerged at an alarming rate. Another had him passing through both Mexico and Central America into South America. According to colleagues, the southern continent was a place of allure for Bierce, one which held up a "beckoning hand…all his life."[128] Such being the case, a story that describes Bierce being captured by an isolated indigenous tribe in the wilds of Mexico seems to make perfect sense. Proponents of this theory go on to suggest that Bierce was boiled alive, and that his "shrunken remains"[129] became objects of worship in ritual "tribal idolatry."[130] A few within this school of thought adopt a less grisly vision of Bierce's interaction with previously undiscovered tribes in the far south. An overlapping theory suggests that he was captured in Central America by a tribe

---

[125] Forrest Gander
[126] The Secular Web
[127] James McWilliams
[128] Today I Found Out, Whatever Happened to Ambrose Bierce? – www.todayIfoundout.com/index.php/2014/03/what-happened-to-ambrose-bierce
[129] Today I Found Out
[130] Today I Found Out

who saw him as a white-haired god. According to these reports, the tribe dressed him in ritualistic animal skins and revered him as a deity, but "forbade him any movement."[131]

A separate group of amateur archaeologists places Bierce and explorer F.A. Mitchell Hedges together in search of the elusive crystal skull in Mayan territory. Hedges, they say, was in the business of stealing Mayan artifacts, and that the two men discovered the skull together, serving as a distant inspiration for latter day archaeologist and adventurer Indiana Jones. They add that Hedges was eventually captured and executed, but no mention is made of Bierce suffering a similar fate. Some believe that the two were taken to Honduras, and others are certain that they were held in a Mayan temple.

The idea that one such as Ambrose Bierce would die of mere pneumonia in his travels, or that he spent 1914 in an insane asylum, seems out of place for such a larger-than-life character. A more lively and heroic view has him fighting in World War I alongside British troops. This is questionable, as the British army was not normally in the habit of taking on elderly foreign activists for major combat missions.

In 1929, a guerilla who claims to have ridden with Villa was interviewed by Adolphe Danziger De Castro, a San Francisco dentist, and he repeated the claim that the chief outlaw killed Bierce himself, not for arguing about war tactics, but merely for drinking too much tequila.

Into the early 21st century, it may be that amateur historian Leon Day is the closest to finding a definitive answer. Day has worked for many years on the Bierce mystery as a devotee and talented researcher. He points with satisfaction to a belief that Bierce "stood behind his works with a gun, not a lawyer,"[132] and that in his effort to make the agony of war stories come alive, "he included the terror and put the glory in its place."[133] Day, like Wilkinson, searched in Mexico for Bierce's remains, and believes that he has very likely found them, along with more pieces of the story to fit into the Bierce puzzle. His supposed itinerary for Bierce was that he visited San Antonio, where officers at Fort Sam Houston purportedly treated him like visiting royalty. In all likelihood, he did cross the border at Laredo, being recognized there by a Mr. Cromell, the editor of the *Mexico City Herald*.

Day agrees with the account of Bierce meeting his death at Sierra Mojada, and suspects that the remains under Padre Leinert's monument are, indeed, his. As one hears Day's story of Bierce's proposed death in further detail, an updated twist holds that Bierce was drinking with two soldiers, and that when the three of them went outside for some target shooting, they asked Bierce to hang the target. He did, but when he turned around, they riddled him with bullets. The report continues to say that Bierce laughed heartily as he went down, a finish worthy of his best stories. Considering his general stance toward life and possible motivation for the journey in the

---

[131] Today I Found Out
[132] James McWilliams
[133] James McWilliams

first place, it may well be true. Some historians still speculate that Bierce was lynched in Sierra Mojada, and it is claimed that a collection of his papers was recovered in the room where he stayed nearby–not the beautifully refined paper to which he had been accustomed, but 10 sheets of rough 5 x 8 lined manuscript.

Author James Robertson, assembling a "lavish"[134] collection of Bierce's *Civil War Writings* years later, took the time to reinvestigate the Danziger De Castro interview in a final search for clues as to the writer's disappearance. His findings were introduced in a *Los Angeles Times* article by Garry Adams, in which the character of the elderly Bierce "drank like a fish, spewed invective like a volcano [and] seemed justly destined for oblivion."[135] However, the author salutes Bierce by calling his decision to enter the maelstrom of the Mexican revolution "a great career move…a masterstroke, [before being] devoured by a historical black hole."[136] The list of investigative bodies in the article was impressive, as the Bierce case stumped Secret Service agents, Pinkerton Detectives, and every other professional investigative force. Robertson, however, endured, although he found the De Castro interview "almost unreadable and self-serving."[137] De Castro's central point taken from the interview, after haranguing Bierce as a hate-monger and womanizer to the guerilla, was not that he drank too much tequila, but that in doing so he became loose-lipped and criticized Villa's brother, which was an intolerable act against his family. The old fighter added, for theatrical effect, that De Castro should not worry, because Bierce would never bother him or his woman again, as "he has passed."[138] Robertson, despite the generally off-putting nature of the De Castro text, admitted that there might be "an odor of authenticity"[139] in the document.

Biographer Vincent Starrett, in his book *Ambrose Bierce*, believes to see a way in which Bierce met death on his own terms. Despite a lack of absolute certainty surrounding the details of his demise, Starrett is certain that it was as adventurous as the rest of the author's life, and that "his death was terribly beautiful and fitting…an appropriate conclusion…he had lived a life of erratic adventure and high endeavor."[140]

Although the location of his remains has not been clearly identified, a marker has been set aside for Bierce's memory at Oakwood Cemetery in Warsaw, Kosciusko County, Indiana.

As for those who felt strongly one way or the other about Bierce as a human being and writer, his disappearance altered very little of public opinion or expression. The "rabid admiration"[141] of his idolaters was as heartily expressed as before, while the "acrid disapproval

---

[134] Garry Adams, Los Angeles Times, June 25, 1991 – www.articles.latimes.com/1991-06-25/news/vw-1440_1_ambrose-bierce
[135] Garry Adams
[136] Garry Adams
[137] Garry Adams
[138] Garry Adams
[139] Garry Adams
[140] Humanities, Edsitement, Edgar Allen Poe, Ambrose Bierce, and the Unreliable Biographies – www.edsitement.neh.gov/lesson-plan/edgar-allen-poe-ambrose-bierce-and-unreliable-biographies

of his detractors"[142] remained unmoved. A personal brand of criticism continued for years after his disappearance by those who lived in his era, in his region of the United States, and by those working in his profession. Like the politics Bierce abhorred, the commentary was always "belligerently partisan."[143]

British critics, slow to approve of Bierce's approach to literature, were less than charitable due to his abusive treatment of Oscar Wilde. An Oxfordian, Walter Richardson, described Bierce as "not a great writer…compared to the really great,"[144] but admitted that his body of work might hold a fascination for a particular type of reader. He also ceded that while Bierce is an obscure figure to most, those who read any of his works generally read more than one. He further predicted, "a small, obscure, but permanent place"[145] for Bierce in American literature. Another native critic deemed Bierce's work as generally "insolent, entertaining, and sometimes courageous."[146]

Bierce appeared close to being a forgotten author among company in which he should have remained a stellar member. The silent film based on his short story *Occurrence at Owl Creed Bridge* also spawned two Twilight Zone episodes on the same story. In 1967, an enlarged edition of *The Devil's Dictionary*, edited by E.J. Hopkins, was published. In 1985, a novel by Carlo Fuentes, *The Old Gringo*, was released, based on Bierce's hypothetical exploits and demise in Mexico. *A Sole Survivor: A Bit of Autobiography* was republished in 1998, and in the following year, Roy Morris published an informative volume employing the Bierce quote, *Alone: in Bad Company*. 2003 saw the publication of *A Much Misunderstood Man: Selected Letters of Ambrose Bierce*. Bierce played the heroic central character in George Kersh's *The Secret of the Bottle*, and an ABC episode of the serial *Lost* was based on a Bierce story.

The best of the new collections is generally thought to be the New Library of America Volume, *Ambrose Bierce: The Devil's Dictionary, Tales, and Memoirs*, but critics caution the modern reader to read but one section or story at a time, as if to imply that if too much is ingested in a short period of time, "the magic wears off."[147] One might be wary of risking the condition Bierce was so proud of offering in his many reviews, that "the cover of this book [was] too far apart."[148]

As a master of suspense, Bierce wrote on the subject of war for most of his adult life, with plot twists reminiscent of the infamous surprises of Henry James. However, other works emerged as well. During the same year of 2003, a perversely delightful volume of stories, entitled *The Parricide Club*, received new publication. In this whimsical cavalcade of parents

---

[141] Paul Fatout, Ambrose Bierce (1842-1914), American Literary Realism, 1870-1910, Vol. 1 No. 1 (Fall, 1967) p. 13
[142] Paul Fatout
[143] Paul Fatout
[144] U.S. Scholarship Repository, University of Richmond, Spring 1939 – www.scholarship.richmond.edu/masters-theses/18/
[145] U.S. Scholarship Repository
[146] Fantastic Fiction, Ambrose Bierce – www.fantasticfiction.com/b/ambrose-bierce/
[147] Terrance Rafferty
[148] Brainy Quotes

murdered by their children in the most ingenious ways, one can see the foreshadowing of *The Addams Family* and other reality-bending examples of the dark side of human nature, such as the European book for children, *Strubelpeter*, a macabre set of lessons that could have come directly from Bierce's imagination.

Since Bierce's actual activities across the border are still a mystery after more than a century, a 2016 novel by Don Swain has attempted fill the void with a quasi-biographical account of what might have happened. It is entitled *The Assassination of Ambrose Bierce: A Love Story*, published by Hippocampus Press. Characters, such as a violent and urge-driven Villa, are vividly brought to life, and one critic remarked that the novel offered the closest thing to a live Ambrose Bierce as one could hope for.

Bierce served as a strong influence on some of the most promising young writers of his day, including George Washington Cable, George Sterling, Stephen Crane, Jack London, and Robert Hemingway. He also helped shape the development of the German (and American) short story.

To categorize Bierce's genre is not overly difficult. However, when one considers the subsets and motivations that produced his best works, there is debate. Eric Solomon refers to him as a "realist and naturalist,"[149] while Daniel Aaron claims he is only a realist because of his war experience. He adds that, in his mind, Bierce is very much a romantic, despite the author's protestations to the contrary. Others omit him from both categories, labeling him under "psychological,"[150] a term that rings as woefully narrow for the task.

Regardless of classification, Gertrude Atherton insisted that "the field was too small for his genius."[151] Modern great, Kurt Vonnegut, took the matter further, declaring that he considers anyone who has not read *The Occurrence at Owl Creek Bridge* to be a "twerp."[152] He describes the work as the finest short story ever written in America, and compares it in quality to Duke Ellington's *Sophisticated Lady* and the Franklin stove.

Colorful characters who obstinately followed a distinctive path are strewn all about history. However, many of the most pugnacious, defiant life views and artistic poses decay into existential pouting when put under the pressure of public judgment. Ambrose Bierce, the "eccentric of human letters,"[153] declared that he cared nothing for such things, and feared little in this life. In the end, he made good on his word. As historians and sleuths of antiquity continue to probe the story of Bierce's disappearance for new clues, one quote from the author's lexicon stands above all the others: "Obscurity is obscurity, but disappearance is fame."[154]

---

[149] Philip Rubens, Robert Jones, Ambrose Bierce: A Bibliographical Essay and Bibliography, American Literary Realism, 1870-1910, University of Illinois Press, Vol. 16 No. 1, Spring, 1983
[150] Philip Rubens
[151] James McWilliams
[152] The Ambrose Bierce Project
[153] M.E. Grenander, Ambrose Bierce, Review by James Bellowe, Twayne Pub., American Quarterly Vol. 24 No. 3, (Aug. 1972), Johns Hopkins University Press, p. 283

Online Resources

Other books about authors by Charles River Editors

Other books about Ambrose Bierce on Amazon

Bibliography

Alangulette.com, Ambrose Bierce – www.alangulette.com/lit/bierce/

Ambrose Bierce.org/timeline8.html

Ambrose Bierce Letters Project, University of Cincinnati – www.libapps.libraries/uc.edu/exhibits/ambrose-bierce-2/

American Literature.com, Ambrose Bierce – www.americanliterature.com/author/ambrose-bierce/bio-books-stories/=

Ballowe, James, Ambrose Bierce, review by M.E. Grenander, Twayne Publicatiions, American Quarterly Vol. 24 No 3 (
August 1972), Johns Hopkins University Press

Brainy Quotes, Ambrose Bierce – www.brainyquote.com/quotes/authors/ambrose_bierce2.html

Casey, John, Fordham Scholarship Online, New Men: Reconstructing the Image of the Veteran in Late Nineteenth-Century American Literature and Culture - 2015

Dr. Weirdre, The Wickedest Man in San Francisco: Ambrose Bierce Historical Essay – www.foundsf.org/index.php?title=The-wickedest-man-in-San-Francisco:_Ambrose_Bierce

Edwards, Tim, eScholarship, University of California, Transnational American Studies – The Real Prayer and the Imaged: The War Against Romanticism in Twain, Howells, and Bierce

Enclyclopaedia Britannica, Ambrose Bierce, Author – www.britannica.com/biography/Ambrose_Bierce

Fantastic Fiction, Ambrose Bierce: - www.fantasticfiction.com/b/ambrose-bierce/

Fatout, Paul, Ambrose Bierce (1842-1914), American Literary Realism, 1870-1910, Vol. I No. I (Fall, 1967)

Galles, Gary, Mises Institute, Ambrose Bierce on Politics (Austrian Economics, Freedom, and

---

[154] Brainy Quote

Peace – www.mises.org/blog/ambrose-bierce-politics

Gander, Forrest, The Paris Review, Brown University, The Many Deaths of Ambrose Bierce, Oct. 17, 2014 – www.theparisreview.org/blog/2014/10/17/very-trustworthy-witnesses/

Goldberg, Steffany Anne, The Smart Set, Pertinent and Impertinent – To the Devil, the New Dictionary at 100 – www.thesmartset.com/article09261101

Guelzo, Allen, Civil War Times Magazine, Historynet – Ambrose Bierce's Civil War: One Man's Morbid Vision – www.historynet.com/ambrose-bierces-civil-war-one-mans-morbid-vision.htm

Humanities Edsitement, Edgar Allan Poe, Ambrose Bierce, and the Unreliable Biographers – www.neh.gov/lesson-plan/edgar-allan-poe-ambrose-bierce-unreliable-biographers

IMDb, Ambrose Bierce Biography – www.imdb.com/name/nm0081549/bio?ref_=nm_ov_bio_sm#trivia

Johnson, Marianne, S., Gettysburg College – A Jaded Romantic: Uncovering the True Nature of Ambrose Bierce

Joshi, S.T., Schultz, David E., Introduction to A Sole Survivor: Bits of Autobiography by Ambrose Bierce, Knoxville, University of Tennessee, 1998

Kelly Debra, the Knowledge Nuts, Dec. 12, 2013, the Mysterious Disappearance of Ambrose Bierce – www.knowledgenuts.com/2013/12/12/the-mysterious-disappearance-of-ambrose-bierce

Library of America, Ambrose Bierce: The Devil's Dictionary, Tales & Memoirs – www.loa.org/books/347-the-devils-dictionary-tales-memoirs

McWilliams, Jim, Dickinson State University, NY Times, Ambrose Bierce's Civil War, Dec. 17, 2013 – www.opinionator.blogs.nytimes.com/2013/12/17/ambrosebierces-civil-war/?_r=o

McWilliams, James, Devil in the Details, Why is 'Talented Amateur Historian' Leon Day Obsessed with the Death of Ambrose Bierce? May 17, 2002, Austin Chronicle

Morris, Roy, Oxford Scholarship Online, Ambrose Bierce, Alone: In Bad Company – www.oxfordscholarship.com/view/10.1093/acprof:050/9780195126280.001.0001/acprof-9780195126280

Morris, Roy, The Washington Post, Ambrose Bierce – www.washingtonpost.com/wp-srv/style/longterm/books/chap1/bierce.htm

Morrone, Peter, The Midwest Quarterly, Questia, The Ethics of Moral Resistance: Ambrose

Bierce and General William B. Hazen

New World Encyclopedia, Ambrose Bierce – www.newworldencyclopedia.org/entry/Ambrose_Bierce

O'Brien, Matthew C., Ambrose Bierce and the Civil War: 1865, American Literature Vol. 48 No. 3 (Nov. 1976) Duke University Press

Patrick, John, Murphy, Michael, The Secular Web, 1999, Ambrose Bierce – www.infidels.org/library/modern/john_murphy/ambrosebierce.html

Rafferty, Terrance, New York Times: Ambrose Bierce: The Man and His Demons, Oct. 28, 2011 – www.nytimes.com/2011/10/30/books/review/ambrose-bierce-the-man-and-his-demons.html?_r=o

Rubens, Philip, Jones, Robert, Ambrose Bierce: A Bibliographic Essay and Bibliography, American Literary Realism, 1870-1910, University of Illinois Press, Vol. 16 No. 1 (Spring 1983)

Spartacus Educational, Ambrose Bierce – www.sparacus-educational.com/USABierce.htm

Swain, Don, The Assassination of Ambrose Bierce: A Love Story, Hippocampus Press – www.hippocampuspress.com/mythos-and-other-authors/fiction/the-assassination-of-ambrose-bierce

Swain, Don, The Ambrose Bierce Site, Ambrose Bierce Chronology – donswain.com/bierce-chronology.html

The Ambrose Bierce Project, Works – www.ambrosebierce.org/works.htm

The Free Online Library, Ambrose Bierce (1842-1914) – www.bierce.thefreeonlinelibrary.com

The Literature Network, The Crime at Pickett's Mill – www.online-literature.com/bierce/1991

The Yellow Site, Ambrose Bierce – www.kinginyellow.wikia.com/wiki/Ambrose-Bierce

Today I Found Out, Whatever Happened to Ambrose Bierce? – www.todayIfoundout.com/index/php/2014/03/whatever-happenedambrose-bierce/

US Scholarship Repository, University of Richmond, Spring 1939 – www.scholarship.richmond.edu/masters-theses/18/

Made in the USA
Monee, IL
11 May 2023